Little Cloud
and the Bully Clouds

Maryln Appelbaum and Stephanie Catlett
Illustrated by Stephanie Catlett

Thank You From Maryln:
Thank you so much to all of you that work with children and make a difference.
Thank you Stephanie for your hard work and for your great idea and illustrations that brought Little Cloud to life.
Thank you to our wonderful Appelbaum team led by Marty who work so hard to make this world a better place for children.

Thank You from Stephanie:
To the Appelbaum Training Institute, educators, and child care providers everywhere.
You enrich the lives of children with fun and innovative ideas
that make learning enjoyable. You are making a difference, thank you.
To my family and friends, your love and support overwhelms me, thank you.
You all inspired me to bring Little Cloud to life.
Thank you Marty Appelbaum and Maryln Appelbaum for the honor of sharing this project with you, and for believing in the idea of Little Cloud from the very beginning.
Your gentle guidance and strong encouragement kept the vision of this book alive.
Thank you for the privilege of working with you.

Library of Congress Cataloging-in-Publication Data Available
# # # # # # # # # #

Published by Appelbaum Training Institute, Inc.
104 Industrial Boulevard, Suite A
Sugar Land, TX 77478
Text copyright © 2013 by Maryln Appelbaum and Stephanie Catlett
Illustrations copyright © 2013 by Stephanie Catlett
Distributed in USA by Appelbaum Training Institute, Inc.
104 Industrial Boulevard, Suite A
Sugar Land, TX 77478
Printed in USA
ISBN 978-0-9892990-0-8

This is Little Cloud.
He is soft, and bright white,
and when he is happy, he smiles.

Little Cloud likes to change his shape.
All clouds like to change their shapes,
just like people change their clothes.

Little Cloud floats in the sky all day.
At night he changes his color from
bright white to smoky silver.
Little Cloud is a happy cloud.

One day a group of clouds started to play together. They did not include Little Cloud. Instead they struck him with lightning bolts, poking him and hurting him. They thundered loudly at Little Cloud laughing at him. It made him feel scared.

Little Cloud felt sad. He started to fill up with tears and turn gray, and then he began to rain. He rained, and rained, and rained. That is how clouds cry.

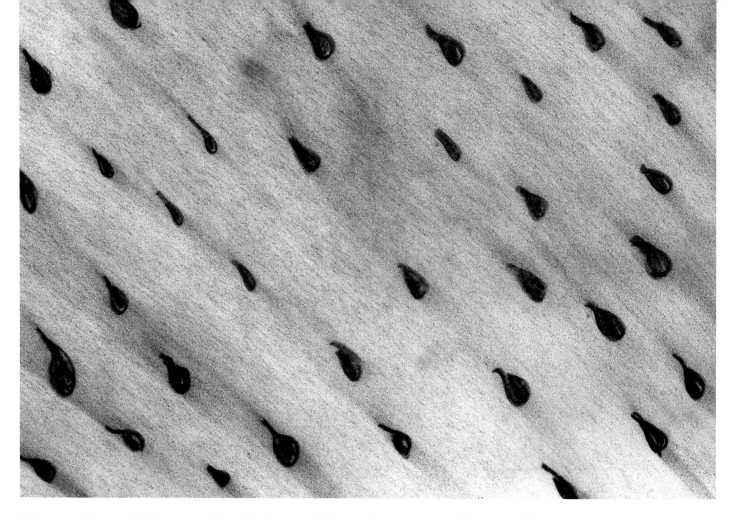

Little Cloud felt all alone. He kept raining tears. He did not understand why the other clouds were so mean. He did not do anything to them. Little Cloud was so very sad.

Little Cloud needed help, so he called out for help. He knew he needed to find a bigger friend to help him.

The Sun is full of bright light and is very kind. The Sun shines on people, and if the Sun sees someone hurting, the Sun wants the hurt to go away.

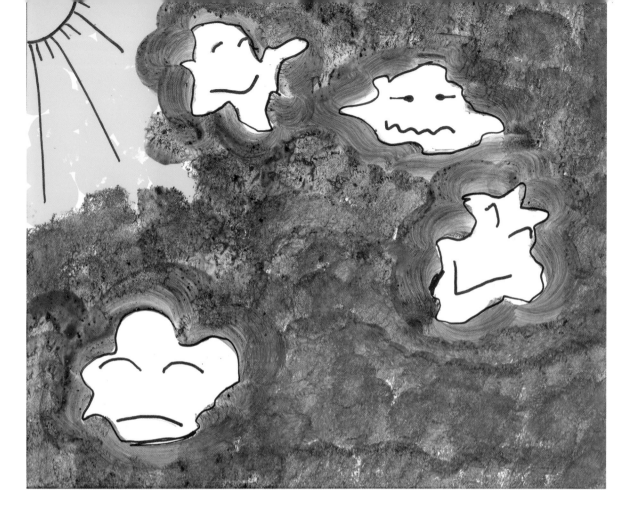

The Sun heard Little Cloud and noticed that the other clouds were bullying Little Cloud.
The Sun said, "This must stop!"

The Sun began to shine so brightly. The bullying
clouds felt the Sun's warm bright rays.
It made them stop hurting Little Cloud,
and the bullying clouds rolled away.

The Sun told Little Cloud about a very special club called the Bully Detective Club.
The Sun is a member of this special club.
The Bully Detective Club needs new members to help children that are bullied.
Little Cloud decided to join the club and be like the Sun and help others that are bullied.

The Sun said, "When you are a Bully Detective, you watch out for your friends. If someone is hurting them or saying mean things, a Bully Detective finds a bigger friend to help."

Little Cloud listened to the Sun and felt the Sun's warmth. It felt so good, just like a big hug. The Sun's rays got warmer and wider. The sunlight began to shine through Little Cloud.

It was nice to have the Sun for a friend. Little Cloud began to smile. Little Cloud's smile got bigger and bigger, so big that beautiful colors started to shine out of him. The colors were vibrant and cheerful, like a great big laugh.

Little Cloud did laugh. He laughed so much that his smile of colors stretched across the sky, creating a beautiful rainbow. Everyone looked up to see Little Cloud. Everyone thought he was so beautiful. Little Cloud smiled more. He felt good. He forgot all about the bullies and kept smiling.

Little Cloud and the Sun have a special message for you. They want you to join the Bully Detective Club.

It's very important to get help when you see friends and other children being bullied.

They want you to be just like the Sun when Little Cloud called out for help.

Here's how to be a Bully Detective.

1. Look for Bully Clues

When children are bullied, they are sad and sometimes very quiet. Ask them if they are okay.

If you see someone saying mean things,
or hitting or hurting someone, those
are clues that someone is being bullied.

2. When you find a Bully Clue,
it's important to tell a bigger friend.

Do not try to solve the Bully problem all by yourself. You need help. Don't be afraid to tell an adult. If the adult doesn't listen to you the first time, tell the adult again. Keep telling adults until you get someone to listen and help.

You can
help others!

You can
be kind!

Being a Bully Detective is an important and serious job. It takes courage. You can be a Bully Detective and help others. You can help others feel warm and sunny inside just like the Sun did for Little Cloud.

You can
be a
Bully
Detective!

You can
make a
difference!

If you're ready to be a Bully Detective and join the club, say,
"I'm going to be a Bully Detective!"

CERTIFICATE OF HONOR

Awarded
with pride

Official Bully Detective

_____

for being
caring and
looking for
BULLY CLUES!